Karen Ma

Bobbin Lace Jewellery

Akacia

Bobbin Lace Jewellery
By Karen Marie Iversen

© 2012 Forlaget Akacia
Skovvænget 1
5690 Tommerup
Denmark
akacia@akacia.dk

Printed at InPrint, Riga, 2012

ISBN: 978-87-7847-118-5

Foreword

In my former book, "Modern Bobbin Lace", I used various thicknesses of Madeira Metallic thread in silver and gold. I was so impressed by the thread that I felt compelled to use it again for jewellery. This resulted in bracelets, necklaces, earrings and also brooches for blouses and shawls.

The techniques used are Milanese inspired and also Idria and Lutac, all of which are described in detail in this book.

Once again I have been supported throughout the whole procedure by the aid of my friend, Bibi Tholstorf, who has tried out the patterns, inspired me and given me the necessary "nudge" when I have been about to give up. She has my grateful thanks.

Happy Lacemaking with my book.

Karen Marie Iversen
Greve, 2012-05-30

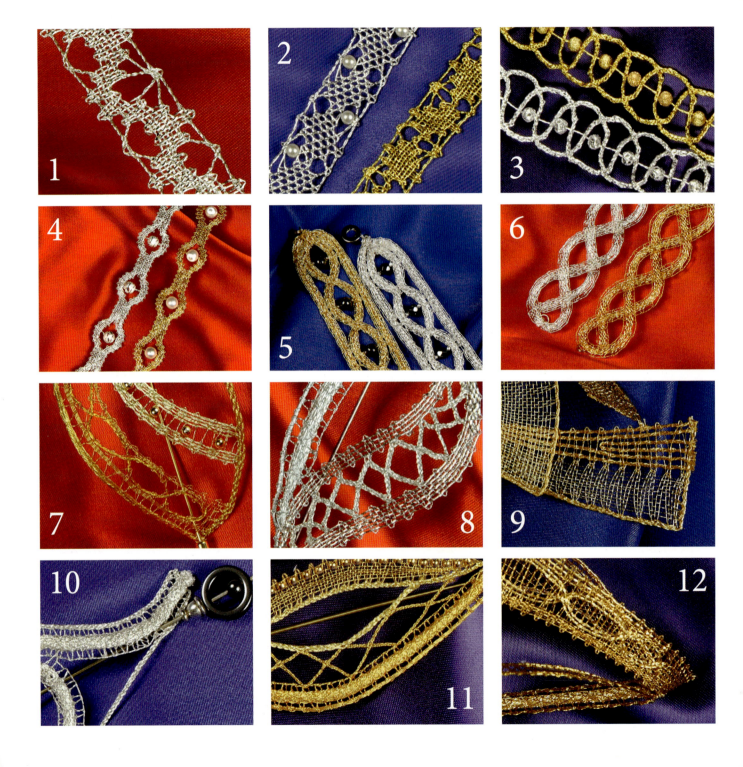

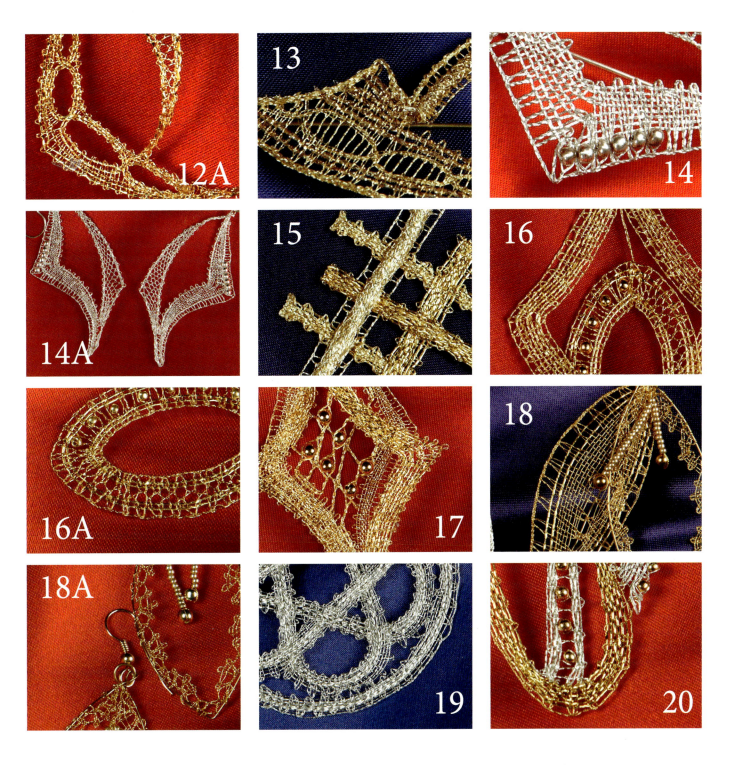

About the lace

In free lace one is not bound by strict routine, regularity of pinholes or the same thickness of thread throughout the work – in fact there are no rules.

In free lace an outline is drawn and then fantasy takes over! Throughout the work decisions are made regarding the density of the lace (i.e. how close the pinholes should be), the direction of work/pattern and the choice of thread colour and thickness.

All the designs in this book have started with an outline, and I set to work from there employing techniques from Duchesse Lace and fillings from Milanese Lace.

In Milanese Lace, tapes are made with different fillings but the tapes never cross each other. As the work proceeds, sewings are made to link the tapes.

A variety of plaits are used to link the elements of the pattern, and sometimes beads are added. The final lace pattern is achieved after several trials and errors in combining fillings, thread qualities and lace techniques.

The models are stiffened with Belgian stiffener from the Kantcentrum in Belgium.

Colour Code

Lilac: linen stitch
Red: whole stitch
Green: half stitch
Black: prick/twists
plaits/gimp

Adding a helping thread and finishing off

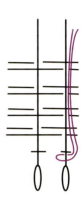

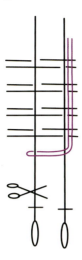

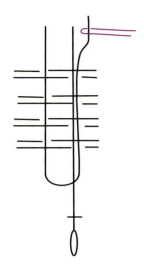

Introduce the helping thread to the right hand bobbin of the pair ca. 5 rows before finishing.

Remove the helping thread from the right hand bobbin. Cut the left hand bobbin thread ca.10cm from the lace and place the cut thread through the loop of the helping thread.

Pull the cut thread up through the lace using the helping thread.

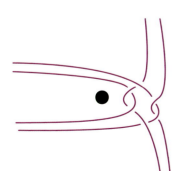

Turn Stitch

Cross, twist, twist, cross and position the pin on the inside of the 2 pairs.

Duchesse Roll

Gather all the bobbins in a bundle. Take one bobbin and make catch stitches around the bundle.

Venetian Plait

2 pairs of workers and 2 pairs of passives/2 thread bundles. Twist the workers around the 2 passives/ bundles of threads. Make a linen stitch with the middle 2 pairs (i.e. the workers). Repeat and tension the threads.

Princess Stitch

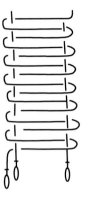

Take one thread from the worker pair and gather the remaining threads in 2 bundles. Weave the worker thread alternatively over and under the bundles. Tension the threads after each row. The worker thread should conceal the bundles.

Crossing of two plaits using a big linen stitch

Each pair is worked as a single thread.

1. Pair 2 is crossed over pair 3.
2. Pair 2 is crossed over pair 1 and pair 4 is crossed over pair 3.
3. Finally pair 2 is crossed over pair 3.

Linking a plait with a motif

Pair 2 from the plait joins with the motif by working a whole stitch.

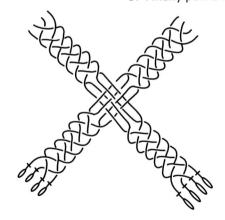

Finishing with a clasp

Gather all the pairs in a plait of approx. 3cm. and tie off the threads. A clasp is placed on the plait, which is folded back over the lace and stitched in place.

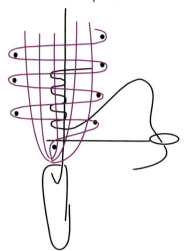

Inserting beads between two linen stitch sections

Place the bead on a crotchet hook. The workers from the left hand side are pulled through the bead. Insert the workers from the right hand side through the loop and tension the threads.

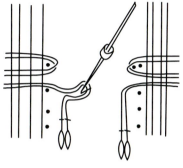

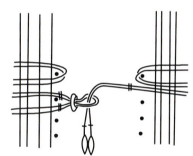

Make sewings into the lower bar

The bar is the section of thread between the passive pair and the edge pair. The diagram illustrates a sewing into the lower bar.

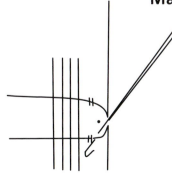

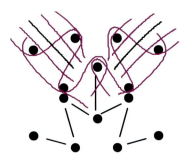
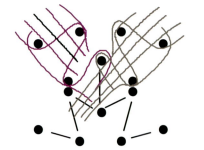

1. The outer workers are worked through each tape and meet with a linen stitch. The pin is positioned.

2+3. Work the inner pairs in linen stitch from right to left and tension the threads.

4. The outer pairs are worked through each tape. The pin is positioned, and the bands continue separately.

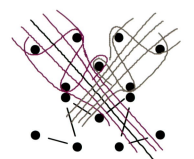
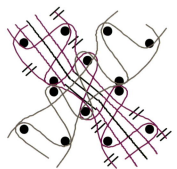

Starting with open pairs

Hang two twisted pairs over a pin. Lay the remaining pairs open under the pin. Work the right hand pair from the pin through the all the right side open pairs, and then do the same for the left side.

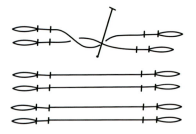
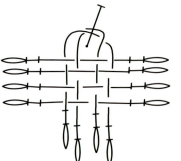

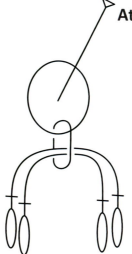

Attaching a ring for a clasp

Position a pin at the top of the pricking and hang two open pairs over the pin. Place both pairs through the O-ring, and form a hitch over the ring by placing the 2 pairs through the loop. The clasp fastens to the O-ring.

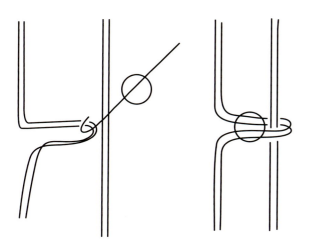

Attaching a bead

Place the bead on a crotchet hook. Pull the thread of bobbin 4 through the bead, and place the thread of bobbin 3 through the loop. Tension the threads.

Chain stitch gimp technique

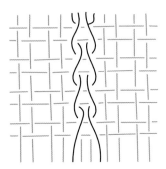

Lift bobbin 2 and 3 and lay the workers over the lower pair. Lay bobbin 2 to the left of 1, and bobbin 3 to the right of 4.

Twisted gimp technique

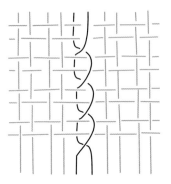

Lift bobbin 2 of the gimp pair, and lay the workers over the lower gimp. Lay bobbin 2 to the left of bobbin 1.

Joining a plait to the workers with turn stitch

Cross thread 4 of the plait over thread 1 of the workers twice. Twist thread 4 and 3 of the plait. Twist thread 1 and 2 of the workers. Cross thread 3 of the plait and thread 2 of the workers twice.

Attaching a bead to a plait

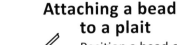

Position a bead on a crotchet hook. Pull the thread of bobbin 4 through the bead, and place bobbin 3 through the loop. Tension the threads.

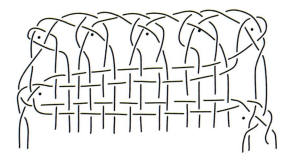

Beginning with a straight edge

Place 2 open pairs on the first pin to the left and twist both pairs. Add an extra pair on a temporary pin to work linen stitch with the first pair. Place the pin between the first and second pair. Remove the temporary pin and tension the threads. Add 2 crossed and open pairs on each of the remaining pins. Work linen stitch with pair 3 from the first pin and pair 1 from the second pin. Remove the pin and replace between the 2 pairs. Continue in this way to the last pin where only one pair is added. Work back through all the pairs in linen stitch.

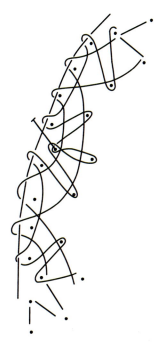

Working twice into a pin

With this pin marking, the same pin is used twice. The passive pairs keep the curve in shape.

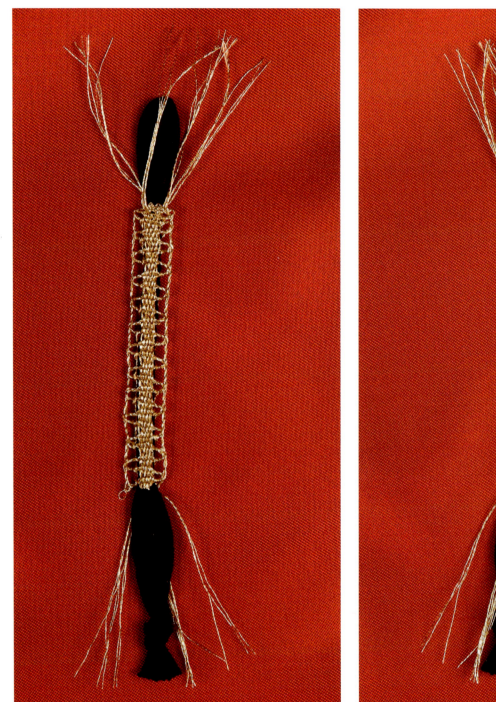
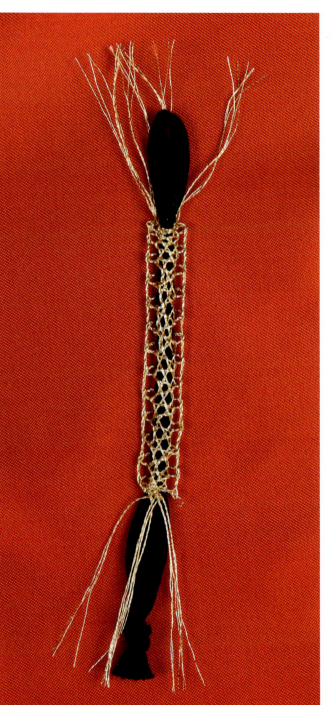

1.

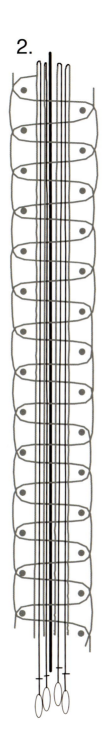

2.

3.

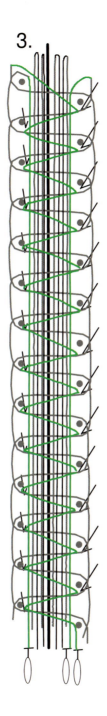

← Front
← Back

Working Lutac

The origin of the name, Lutac, is uncertain. I have knowledge of 2 versions. One is that a French lady, Mm. Lutac, worked this type of lace. The version that I find most credible is that the word, Lutac, can mean an overcoat. The base of Lutac is linen stitch on which a bundle of filling threads is laid and concealed by a half stitch "coat".

1. Using 7 pairs, work in linen stitch to the end, with straight edges on both sides. Turn the pillow.

2. Place the filling threads on a pin above the work. Twist the filling threads together a little so that they are not too bulky, and hold the ends together with tape.

3. Each of the edge pairs plus a passive pair is laid aside for future use. The remaining 3 passive pairs work in half stitch over the bundle of threads, and sewings are made to the lower bars at the edges. When the Lutac is complete the pairs are tied off, and the filling threads are cut off close to both edges.

How to begin designing a motif

I am often asked, "Where do you get the ideas for your lace patterns?" This is difficult to answer, but in daily life I cannot resist looking at objects and shapes, which might produce a lace pattern. This can be a flower, an attractive corner of a book or a piece of wood. Sometimes I simply sit with a pencil and doodle. There are endless possibilities for inspiration.

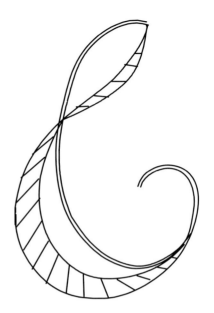

When a suitable shape is produced, I then consider which type of lace can enhance the shape.

Two suggestions are illustrated for a motif. The wider band can either be worked as a Venetian Plait or in Princess Stitch.

The Venetian Plait is not as dense as the Princess Stitch. It is possible to increase the distance between the double lines and instead work Lutac technique (see page 15). Try to think differently. Sometimes a plait along the outer edge can really enhance the lace. Sometimes the motif can be improved by finally working a Duchesse roll to make the contours really sharp. In some cases a patterned tape filling gives an attractive result, or use Lutac technique to achieve a raised effect. One should simply start with threads and pins. The colour and effect of the thread are of great importance. A piece of lace can be "killed" by thread of the wrong thickness or colour. It is necessary to make several trials for each pattern, and it is a great help to have a lace friend to watch over your shoulder during the process. In most cases, constructive criticism is beneficial.

To illustrate what I mean, I have used lace pattern no. 12.

Section 1:
Here I have created a pattern in the tape. Inspiration can be found in Patricia Read and Lucy Kincaid's books, "Milanese Lace: An Introduction" and "New Braids and Designs in Milanese Lace". These books illustrate many different patterns for tape lace. However, the patterns of my tape lace are not from a book. I have chosen to insert 2 gimp threads and these together with twists create decorative holes in the lace. The gimp thread can be thicker than the recommended thread or of another matching colour. I chose a thick glossy thread for the outer passive pair. In addition, a plait or roll can be made on the outer edge. In this model the edge is worked as pin under one pair.

Section 2, Lutac:
I was told that there are 2 explanations as to why the technique is called Lutac. One is the name of the French lady who made this type of lace and the other version, which I prefer, is that Lutac means an overcoat.
See the detailed drawing on page 15.
In Lutac, the base is worked first in linen stitch, with straight edges. After completing the base the

lace pillow is turned. A bundle of filling threads (enough to form a raised curve) is fixed in position and laid over the base. The number of threads in the bundle should be sufficient to form a raised curve without covering the edges of the base. With only 3 pairs in half stitch, the filling is visible and it is therefore important that the colour of the filling compliments the rest of the Lutac lace, but at the same time the colour should be different. Using 3-4 pairs from the linen stitch base, half stitch is worked over the filling threads, and sewings are made into the lower bars of the base edges. See the detailed drawing on page 9. The filling lies over the base keeping the edges free. The edges cannot support themselves and are strengthened with a Duchesse Roll, which uses threads from the extra pairs and a pair of padding threads. There is a detailed drawing on page 8.

Section 3:

Here I have created a "thin transparent" appearance with a special finishing on the right hand side. It is formed with a plait in a thicker thread. It is important that the plait lies very close to the edge of the lace; i.e. rather 1 plait stitch too little than one too many between the join of the tape and the plait.

In this tape there is also a thicker thread at each side in order to strengthen the fragile half stitch ground.

Section 4:

Here I have used 1 pair with thicker thread and one pair with thinner thread for the outer 2 pairs. The thicker pair is outermost and the thinner pair is innermost. The pairs are added open (see the detailed drawing on page 10). The tape is worked with an even number of pairs on the outer edge and one pair in half stitch in the middle. This is a simple variation, which I really like.

The lace sections must be joined and the choice is individual regarding the appearance of the lace. I chose to use the Lutac section as the base, and then turned and twisted the other 3 sections in towards the Lutac section. The sections are sewn together to produce the neatest appearance.

My combination might not appeal to everyone, but I take great pleasure in seeing new combinations and different ideas developing from my patterns. Let your fantasy lead the way.

Enjoy!

No. 1
Bracelet

Thread: gold or Silver

Madeira Metallic Gold 33 Art. no. 9809 no.12
(3 ply)

or

Silver Art. no. 9809 no. 12
(passive pair)

Madeira Metallic Gold 43 Art. no. 9807 no. 6
(thick shiny thread)

or

Silver Art. no. 9807 no. 6
(workers)

1 clasp
7 pairs in all

Begin by placing the clasp as shown (see the detailed diagram page 11).
The tape is worked in linen stitch. Follow the working diagram, and be precise with the twists.
Finishing:
Form a plait with 8 threads. The plait is used to secure the opposite part of the clasp. The remaining threads are tied off.

The lace is stiffened.

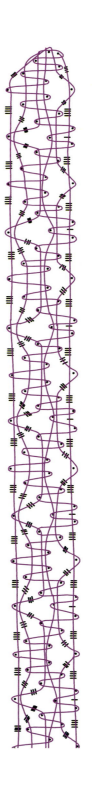

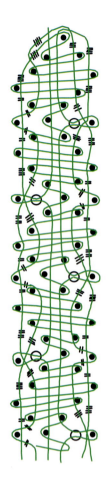

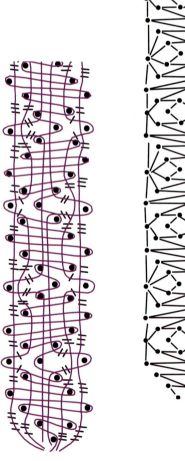

No. 2
Bracelet

Thread: gold or Silver
Madeira Metallic Gold 43 Art.no. 9809 no. 6
or
Silver Art.no. 9809 no. 6

9 of 4mm beads
7 pairs in all

The lace is worked in linen or half stitch, with or without beads.

Attach the first pairs to the eye of the clasp (see detailed diagram page 11) and attach the clasp to the lace pillow.
Follow the working diagram
The bracelet without beads is worked in linen stitch with twists as indicated.
For the bracelet with beads, they are added as indicated on the working diagram. Finish the lace with 4 pairs in a plait. The remaining pairs are tied off, and the opposite part of the clasp is secured to the plait.

The lace is stiffened.

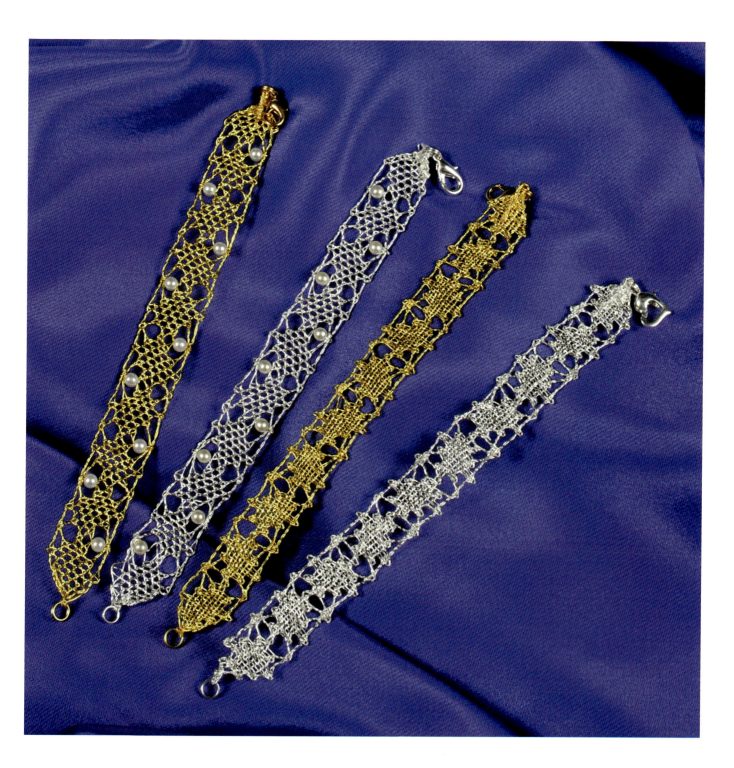

No. 3
Plaited bracelet and earrings

Thread: gold or Silver
Madeira Metallic Gold 43 Art.no. 9807 no. 6
or
Silver Art.no. 9807 no. 6

6 pairs in 3 plaits and 1 thread with beads.
15 of 3mm beads

There is no working diagram for this pattern.

Begin with the first 2 plaits hung in open pairs. Attach one part of the clasp.
Work these plaits until the 3rd plait has to be added and also the thread with 15 beads.
Continue with the plaits and they meet with a "big" linen stitch (see detailed diagram page 8).
Weave the thread with beads through the plaits, pushing a bead into place as indicated on the pricking.
Finish off the plaits with knots or 2 linen stitches.
Use 4 threads to form the plait for attaching the other part of the clasp. The remaining threads are cut off.

The lace is stiffened.

The earrings are worked in the same way.

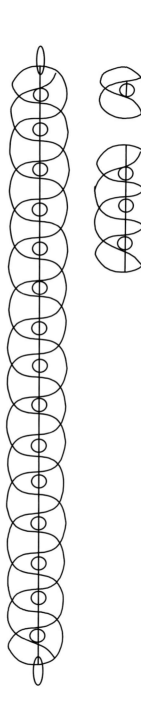

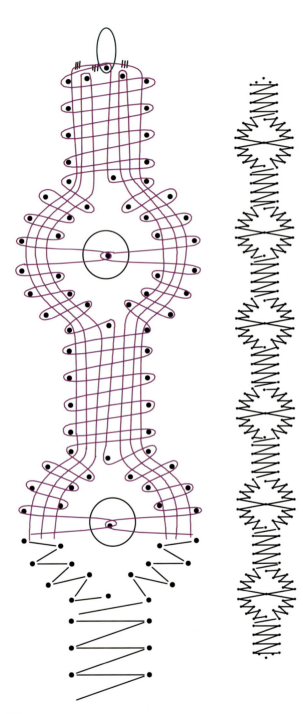

No. 4
Bracelet with beads (bubbles)

Thread: gold or Silver
Madeira Metallic Gold 43 Art.no. 9807 no. 6
(thick, shiny thread)

or

Silver Art.no. 9807 no. 6
(passive pair).

Madeira Metallic Gold 7 Art.no. 9842 nr. 40
(thin thread)

or

Silver Art.no. 9842 no. 40
(workers).

4mm beads
4 pairs thick shiny thread (passives), 4 pairs thin thread (workers). 8 pairs in all.

Begin with 2 pairs of thin thread hung in open pairs on the middle pin (workers). Attach one part of the clasp. 4 passive pairs of shiny thread are added on the pins immediately below. Add an additional pair at each outer edge. Follow the working diagram and insert beads as indicated.

Finishing
Use a helping thread on 2 pairs of passives with thick thread, to the right and left of the middle. The pairs with thin thread are knotted off. The last 2 pairs of thick shiny thread are plaited ca. 1½ cm. for attaching to the other part of the clasp.

The lace is stiffened.

No. 5
Bracelet with beads

Thread: Gold or Silver
Madeira Metallic Gold 43 Art.no. 9807 no. 6
(thick shiny thread)

or

Silver Art.no. 9807 no. 6
(gimp thread)

Madeira Metallic Gold 33 Art.no. 9809 no. 12
(3ply)

or

Silver Art.no. 9809 no. 12
(passive pairs)

Madeira Metallic Gold 3 Art.no. 9842 no. 40
(thin thread)

or

Silver Art.no. 9842 no. 40
(workers)

Total pairs: 14
7 of 6mm beads and 14 wire crimps

Begin with open pairs and attach one part of the clasp.
On each band the pairs are added as follows:
2 pairs Gold 3, 1 pair Gold 33, 2 pairs Gold 43 in chain stitch gimp technique (see detailed diagram page 12), 1 pair Gold 33 and finally 1 pair Gold 3. Follow the working diagram and add beads as indicated.

Finishing
Knot off all pairs except the outer pairs of Gold 33, which are firmly plaited. The other part of the clasp is attached to the plait.

The lace is stiffened.

Diagrams for no. 5

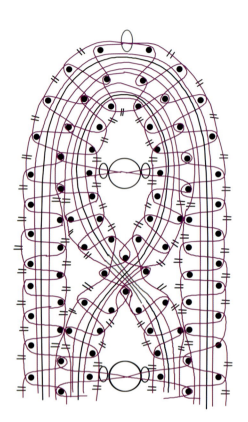

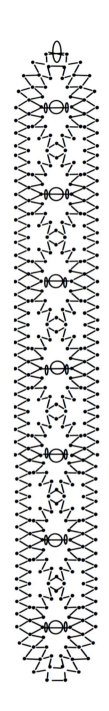

No. 6
Bracelet of 3 interwoven bands

Thread: Gold or Silver
Madeira Metallic Gold 43 Art.no. 9807 no. 6
(thick, shiny thread)

or
Silver Art.no. 9807 no. 6
(passive pairs)

Madeira Metallic Gold Art.no. 9842 no. 40
(thin thread)

or
Silver Art.no. 9842 no. 40
(workers)

6 pairs in each band

Begin the lace at the top with open pairs, and attach one part of the clasp. Follow the working diagram, making one band at a time. Work in linen stitch with pin under 2 on both edges. Work the complete band without making sewings. Finish off by weaving the 3 passive pairs into the band. Plait the 3 worker pairs ca. 1½ cm.

Work the other bands in the same way. Stiffen the lace before removing from the pillow. Plait the 3 bands together and using a thin thread, stitch where they cross. Gather the plaits from each band to mount the other part of the clasp. Fold the plaits into the band and stitch in place.

Stiffen the lace where stitching has been made.

No. 7

Brooch, oval in 2 shades

Thread: Gold or Silver
Madeira Metallic Art.no. 9803, col. 3008
(thick thread)

or

Art.no. 9805 col. 5010

Madeira Metallic Gold 33 Art.no. 9809 no. 12
(3ply)

or

Silver Art.no. 9809 no. 12

Madeira Metallic Gold Art.no. 9844 col. 6033 no. 30
(thin thread)

or

Silver Art.no. 9842 no. 40

Madeira Metallic Gold Art.no. 9804, col. 4002
(thick thread)

or

Silver Art.no. 9803, col. 3010

Madeira Metallic Gold 3, Art.no. 9842 no. 40
(thin thread)

or

Silver Art.no. 9842 no. 40

5 of 3 mm beads
1 hatpin ca. 12 cm

Suggestion

Work the big arch with dark thread and the smaller, innermost ach with light thread.

Begin in the following order from the left:
2 pairs thick thread for a plait and 2 pairs thin thread for the workers (straight edge). To the plait add 2 pairs thin thread, which become passives. Add 2 additional pairs of thin thread, which become the workers in the right edge and "partners" for the thick thread to be added later, see the working diagram. Add 4 more pairs of 3ply gold/silver to the plait, to become passives. Follow the working diagram and add 1 pair of thick thread as indicated. The 2 thick threads become "partners" so that 2 pairs are formed of one thick thread and one thin thread.
Add 2 pairs of thin thread as indicated on the diagram.
Where the work splits, another pair of thin thread is added as workers in the left section of the lace.
Beads are added as indicated on the diagram.
A plait is made to meet the 2 completed sections and the pairs from these sections are tied off in the plait.
The plait finally forms a Duchesse Roll with the workers (see detailed diagram page 8).
The roll is secured and the last threads are tied off.

The lace is stiffened.

Diagrams for no. 7

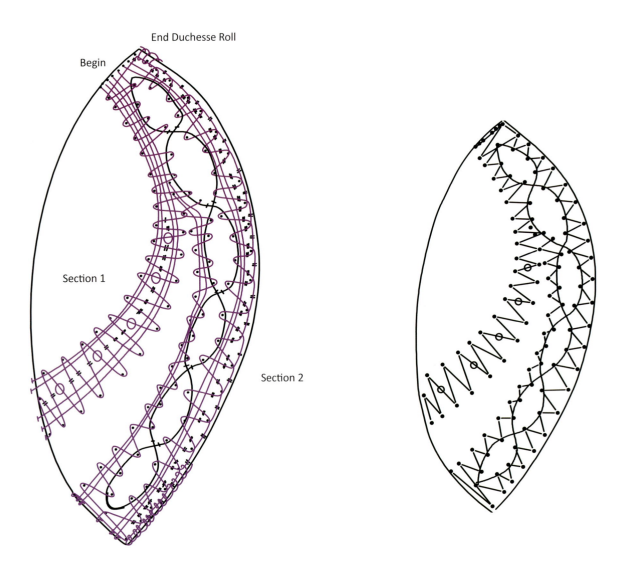

End Duchesse Roll

Begin

Section 1

Section 2

Diagrams for no. 8

Begin

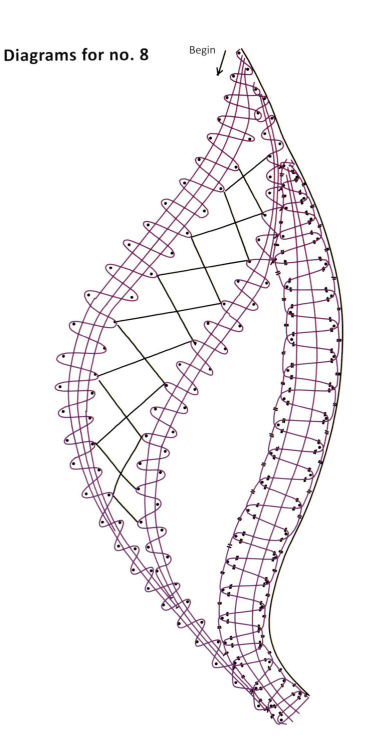

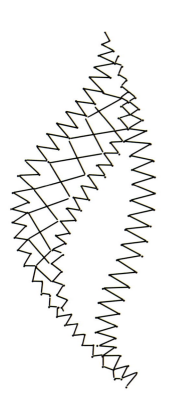

No. 8
Brooch with Lutac

Thread: Gold or Silver

Madeira Metallic Gold 43 Art.no. 9807 no. 6
(thick shiny thread)

or

Silver Art.no. 9807 no. 6
(padding threads and passive pairs)

Madeira Metallic Gold 33 Art.no. 9809 no. 12
(3ply)

or

Silver Art.no. 9809 no. 12
(plait)

Madeira Metallic Gold 7 Art.no. 9842 no. 40
(thin thread)

or

Silver Art.no. 9842 no. 40
(workers)

1 hatpin ca. 12 cm.

Section 1

Begin with a pair of workers in thin thread and 2 pairs of thick shiny thread as passive pairs.

After the second pin an extra passive pair is added. Another worker pair and 2 passive pairs are added as indicated on the working diagram. Continue and follow the diagram. The pairs are removed as indicated, and the last worker pair is left aside to use later in the Lutac base.

The lace filling is made with plaits in Gold 33 or Silver no. 12 (3ply).

Section 2, Lutac

For the Lutac section, add 3 pairs thin thread (workers) and 2 pairs thick thread as the passives, which after working the Lutac base will continue as padding. Extra padding threads are also added. The Lutac is worked according to the detailed diagram on page 15.

When the Lutac is complete, the remaining pairs (ca. 2 pairs thick thread and the workers) are used to form the Duchesse roll on the outer edge.

The pairs are tied off and the lace is stiffened.

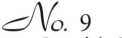

No. 9

Brooch in 3 parts

Thread: Gold or Silver
Fig. 1
Madeira Metallic Gold 33 Art.no. 9809 no. 12
(3ply)

or Silver Art.no. 9809 no. 12
(plait)

Madeira Metallic Gold 43 Art.no. 9807 no. 6
(thick shiny thread)

or Silver Art.no. 9809 no. 6
(passive pairs)

Madeira Metallic Gold 7 Art.no. 9842 no. 40
(thin thread)

or Silver Art.no. 9842 no. 40
(workers)

Fig. 2
Madeira Metallic Gold Art.no. 9803 col.3008
(thick thread)

or Silver Art.no. 9803 col. 3010
(half thickness i.e. 3 strands)

Madeira Metallic Gold 7 Art.no. 9842 no. 40
(thin thread)

or Silver Art.no. 9842 no. 40
(7½ pairs)

Fig. 3
Madeira Metallic Gold Art.no. 9803 col.3008
(thick thread)

or Silver Art.no. 9803 col.3010
(half thickness i.e. 3 strands)

Madeira Metallic Gold 33 Art.no. 9809 no. 12
(3ply)

or Silver Art.no. 9809 nr. 12
(plait)

Madeira Metallic Gold 7 Art.no. 9842 nr. 40
(thin thread)

or Silver Art.no. 9842 nr. 40
(workers and passive pairs)

1 hatpin ca. 12 cm.

Begin Fig. 1 with 3 pairs of 3 ply thread on the first pin together with 1 pair workers (thin thread). Add 8 passives (thick shiny thread) and follow the working diagram. Remove pairs as indicated. Turn the plait at the right edge with a turn stitch (cross, twist, twist, cross and place the pin under 3 pairs), see working diagram. The pairs are removed as indicated and the remaining pairs left for later use.

Begin Fig. 2 with a pair having one thick and one thin thread. Add the remaining pairs according to the working diagram. Work in linen stitch with turn stitch at the edge (cross, twist, twist cross and pin under 2). Pairs are removed as indicated. Leave the thick thread and the workers for later use.

Fig. 3 uses the pairs that have been left aside as indicated in the working diagram. The plaits from Fig. 1 continue on the right edge. The thick pair is in the left edge (pin under 1) and the thin pair continues on the right edge out to the plait. Add another 2 pairs thick thread on the left section and more new pairs as indicated. Finish off with a plait and stiffen the lace.

Diagrams for no. 9

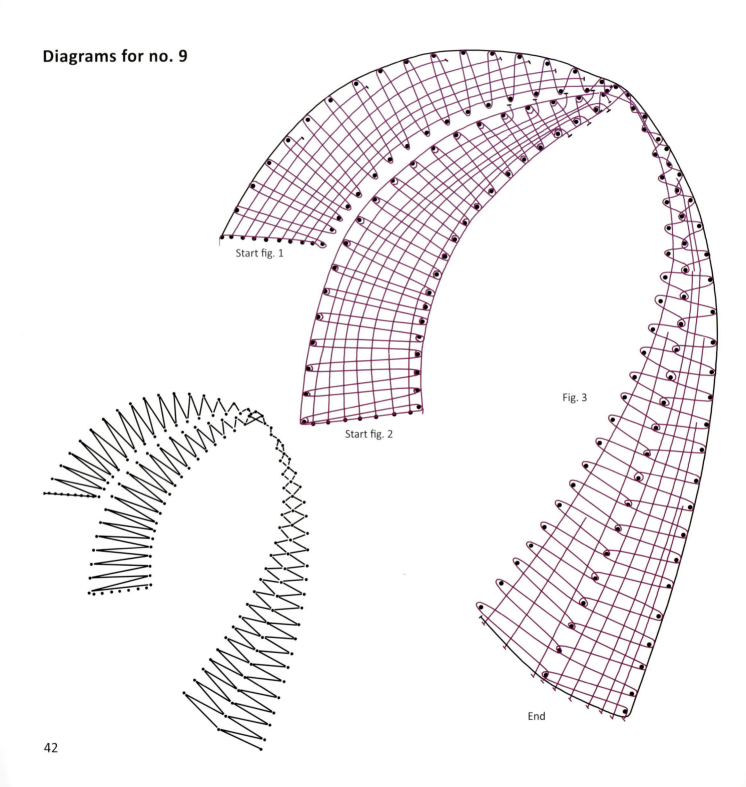

Start fig. 1

Start fig. 2

Fig. 3

End

42

Diagrams for no. 10

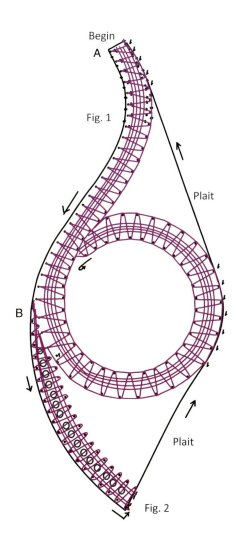

Begin

A

Fig. 1

Plait

B

Plait

Fig. 2

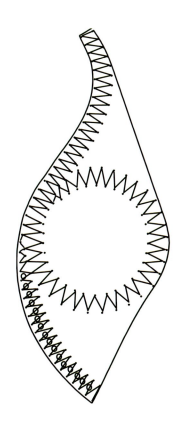

No. 10
Lutac Music

Thread: Gold or Silver

Madeira Metallic Gold 33 Art.no. 9809 no. 12
(3ply)

or

Silver Art.no. 9809 no. 12
(plait)

Madeira Metallic Gold 7 Art.no. 9842 no. 40
(thin thread)

or

Silver Art.no. 9842 no. 40
(workers and passive pairs)

Madeira Metallic Gold Art.no. 9804 col.4002
(thick thread)

or

Silver Art.9803 col.3010
(padding of ca. 10 threads)

16 of wire crimps in gold/silver
1 hatpin ca. 12 cm.

Begin at A with 2 pairs for the plait. Add 6 pairs thin thread to the plait for the Lutac base. Follow the working diagram. Work turn stitch at the left edge to join the plait and the base.

At B add 2 pairs thin thread of which one pair continues in the Lutac base as the 3rd worker pair, and one pair continues in fig. B. Add 2 more pairs in fig.2 as indicated. Add wire crimps in fig.B as indicated in the working diagram.

Continue the plait and remove the pairs in the plait from fig. B. Leave the plait pairs aside. Continue the Lutac as described in the detailed instructions for Lutac.

The pairs left aside from the plait then continue in a plait, making sewings as indicated. Finish off with catch stitch.

Stiffen the lace.

No. 11

Brooch with Lutac and wire crimps

Thread: Gold or Silver

Madeira Metallic Gold 33 Art.no. 9809 no. 12
(3ply)

or

Silver Art.no. 9809 no. 12
(plait)

Madeira Metallic Gold Art.no. 9844 col.6033 no.
30
(thin thread)

or

Silver Art.no. 9842 no. 40
(workers and passives)

Madeira Metallic Gold Art.no. 9803 col.3008
(thick thread)

or

Silver Art.no. 9803 col. 3010
(padding)

24 of wire crimps
1 hatpin ca. 12 cm.

Begin with 2 pairs 3ply and work a plait to start 1. Add 5 pairs thin thread as indicated on the working diagram. The plait and workers meet in a turn stitch. Complete section 1. Remember to add the wire crimps on the left side. Leave the pairs aside to be concealed in the final Lutac.

Section 2 Lutac

In the Lutac base use 3 worker pairs and 3 passive pairs, all in thin thread. Follow the detailed diagram page 15, and remember the twists.
When the Lutac has been completed, the thick threads are laid aside for later use and the thin threads are used for the Duchesse Roll on the outermost edge.

Padding

In section 3 use 2 pairs 3ply thread for the thick plait and 2 x2 pairs thin threads for the thin plaits, which meet with a "big" linen stitch. Follow the working diagram.
Before stiffening the lace, finish off all the thread ends by darning most of them into the Lutac section. Remember that the right side is upwards on the pillow.

Diagrams for no. 11

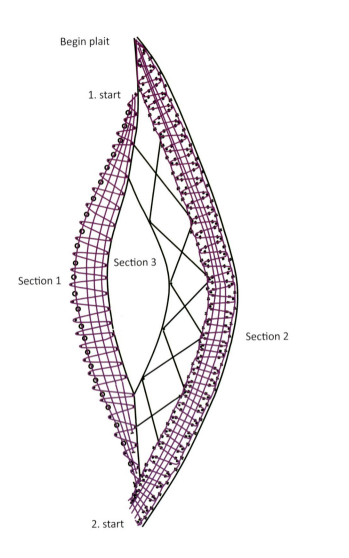

Begin plait

1. start

Section 3

Section 1

Section 2

2. start

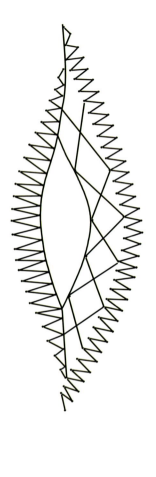

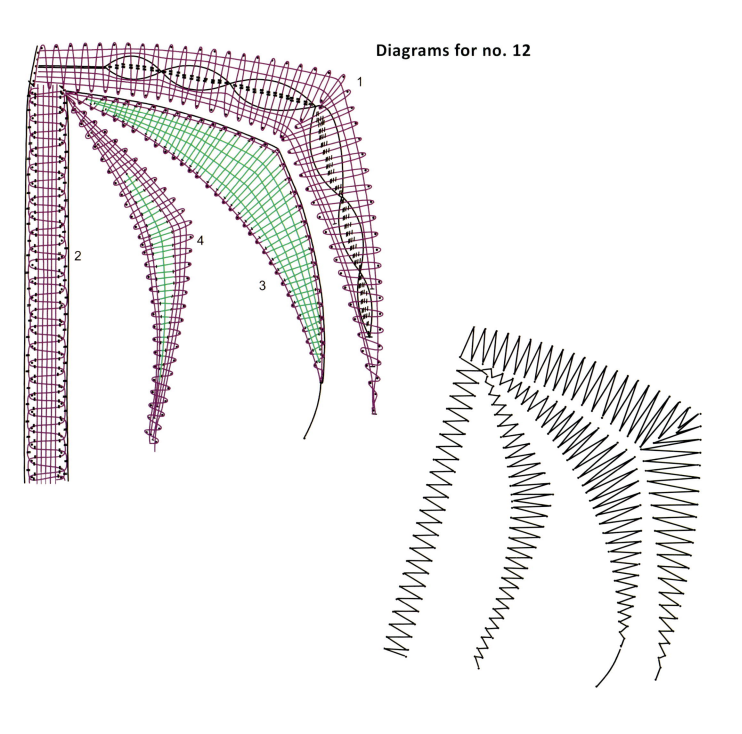

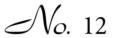 # *No.* 12
4-part Brooch with Lutac band

Thread: Gold or Silver
Madeira Metallic Gold Art.no. 9804 col. 4002
(thick thread)

or

Silver Art.no. 9803 col.3010
(padding)

Madeira Metallic Gold 8 Art.no. 9842 no. 40
(thin thread)

or

Silver Art.no. 9842 no. 40
(workers and passive pairs)

Madeira Metallic Gold 43 Art.no. 9807 no. 6
(thick, shiny thread)

or

Silver Art.no. 9807 no. 6
(plait and passive pair)

Madeira Metallic Gold 33 Art.no. 9809 no. 12
(3ply)

or

Silver Art.no. 9809 no. 12
(passive pairs)

1 hatpin ca. 12 cm

Section 1
Add the pairs from left to right: 4 pairs thin thread (one of which is the workers) and then 2 pairs of 3ply, 1 pair thin thread and 1 pair thick shiny thread. Follow the working diagram and remember the twists inside the "bubbles". Remove pairs as indicated and finish off with knots. Leave one thread aside for stitching together.

Section 2
Lutac: Add 8 pairs thin thread for the Lutac base. Work the Lutac using 12 threads for padding. Finish off with a Duchesse Roll on both edges (see the detailed diagram page 8).

Section 3
Add 2 pairs thick shiny thread for the plait on the right edge, together with 1 pair thin thread as the workers. Then add 2 pairs 3ply (1 to the right and 1 to the left). The thin pairs are added as indicated in the working diagram. Work linen stitch on the left side and turn stitch to link the plaits on the right side. Follow the working diagram and finish off with plaits and knots. Leave one thread for stitching together.

Section 4
Form a pair with one thick thread and one thin thread at the right and left hand edge and add a worker pair in thin thread. Add another thin pair as indicated and follow the working diagram. Finish off with knots and catch stitch. Leave one thread for stitching together.

Stiffen the lace and stitch together.

No. 12A
Earrings to match no. 12

Thread: Gold or Silver

Madeira Metallic Gold 7 Art.no. 9842 no. 40
(thin thread)

or

Silver Art.no. 9842 n. 40
(workers and passive pairs)

Madeira Metallic Gold 43 Art.no. 9807 no. 6
(thick, shiny thread)

or

Silver Art.no. 9807 no. 6
(passive pairs)

Madeira Metallic Gold 33 Art.no. 9809 no. 12
(3ply)

or

Silver Art.no. 9809 no. 12
(passive pairs)

1 pair shepherd hooks

Right: Begin with the section having holes.

Add one pair thick thread and 2 pairs thin thread and follow the working diagram. It can be an advantage to add the pairs for the 2nd part at pin 4 and 5. Leave these pairs aside until later.

Continue with the lace and add 2 more pairs thin thread as indicated, and finally 2 pairs 3ply thread at the first hole. Follow the working diagram and remove pairs as indicated. Tie off the last pairs and secure with a few catch stitches.

Follow the working diagram and continue with the second part. Remove pairs as indicated. Stiffen the finished lace and the pairs can then be cut off close to the work. The small ring from the shepherd hook is attached to the lace.

Work the second earring.

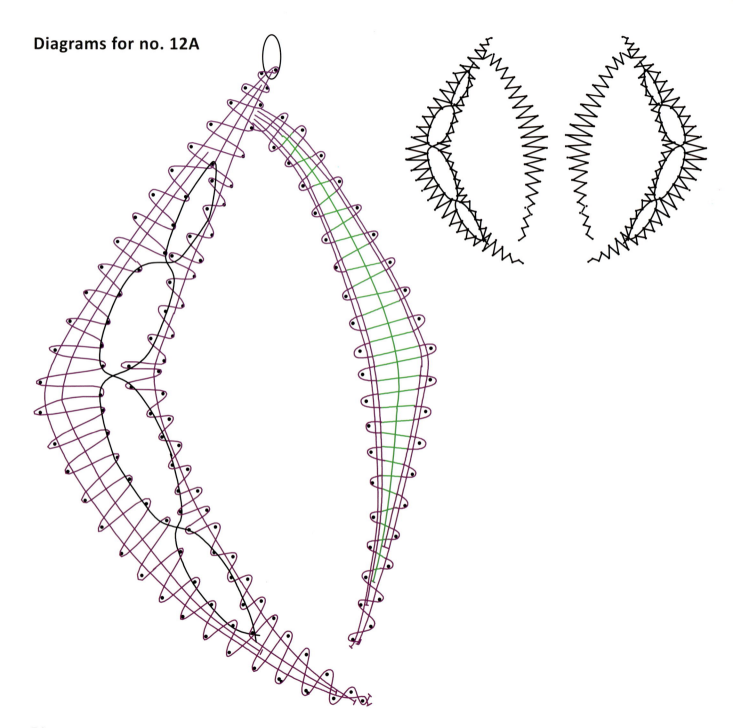

Diagrams for no. 13

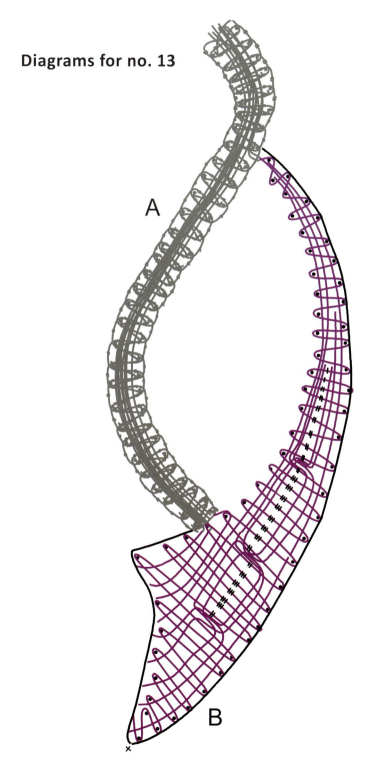

A

B

×

$\mathcal{N}o.$ 13
Lutac with trumpet

Thread: Gold or Silver

Madeira Metallic Gold Art.no. 9810 col. 325
(padding)

or

Silver Art.no. 9804 col. 4010

Madeira Metallic Gold 33, Art.no. 9809, no. 12
(3ply)

or

Silver Art.no. 9809, no. 12

Madeira Metallic Gold 5 no. 40
(thin thread)

or

Art. no. 9842 no. 40

Hatpin ca. 12 cm

Section A, Lutac

Begin with 7 pairs (3 of which are worker pairs and the last 4 are passives). Work the base according to the diagram. Lay 10 padding threads together with the thin passive threads on the base, and work the "overcoat" with the 3 worker pairs. The order of work is 1, 2 and 3 (after the detailed diagram page 15).

Upon finishing the Lutac, the work is turned and the 3 pairs thin thread + 2 pairs thick thread continue in a Duchesse Roll along the outer edge of the Lutac. The remaining pairs are laid aside for later use.

Section B

Add 3 open pairs of 3ply at the point marked * to form a plait along the right and left edges. Position the pairs in the following order:
1 pair 3ply, 4 pairs thin thread, 2 pairs 3ply, and 2 pairs thin thread. Follow the working diagram. The pair from the plait at the right edge and the pairs ending at the Lutac are darned into the Lutac and cut off. The remaining pairs are removed as indicated, and the last pairs plus pairs from the plait are darned into the Lutac and cut off.

The lace is stiffened and mounted on a hatpin.

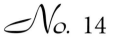

No. 14

Opera house with a Lutac curve

Thread: Gold or Silver

Madeira Metallic Gold 33, Art.no. 9809 no. 12
(3ply)

or

Silver Art.no. 9809 no. 12
(padding)

Madeira Metallic Gold 7, Art.no. 9842 no. 40
(thin thread)

or

Silver Art.no. 9842 no. 40
(thin thread)

6 of 3mm beads
1 hatpin ca. 12 cm

Fig. 1

Begin with 3 pairs 3ply and immediately add another pair. Work pin under 2 on the right edge and pin under 1 on the left edge. Add pairs as indicated and follow the working diagram. To finish fig.1, lay 2 pairs aside as indicated whilst the last 2 pairs continue as a plait in fig. 2.

Fig. 2

Plait to the beginning of fig. 2 and the plait continues on the right edge of the lace. The 2 pairs from fig.1 continue as passives at each side together with 4 more pairs of thin thread in half stitch in the middle of the figure. Remove pairs at the end of fig. 2 as indicated. The plait and one pair of 3ply continue to the beginning of fig. 3.

Fig. 3, Lutac

The 3 pairs of 3ply are the worker pairs in the Lutac. Add 4 pairs thin thread as passives in the middle of the figure.
Work the Lutac as in the detailed diagram. Use the 3ply threads as padding and add more if required. In this model, 16 padding threads are used.

Stiffen the lace and mount on a hatpin.

Diagrams for no. 14

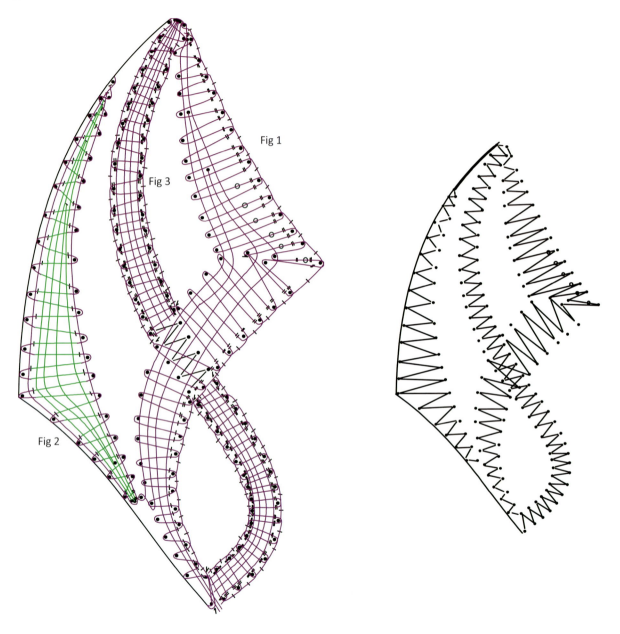

Fig 1

Fig 3

Fig 2

Diagrams for no. 14A

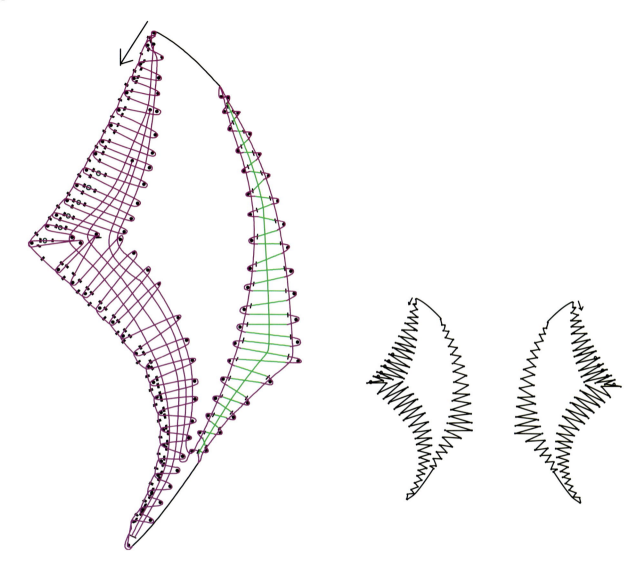

No. 14A

Earrings to match No. 14

Opera house with a Lutac curve

Thread: Gold or Silver
Madeira Metallic Gold 7 Art.no. 9842 no. 40
Or
Madeira Metallic Silver Art.no. 9842 no. 40

6 of wire crimps in gold or silver
1 pair shepherd hooks

Begin with 3 pairs on the first pin and immediately add another pair. Follow the working diagram and add 2 more pairs as indicated. Add the wire crimps as indicated. Lay 2 pairs aside until the next figure. Follow the working diagram and turn with 2 pairs that are plaited to the next figure. At this point the 2 resting pairs are included and continue in the lace.
Finish with 3 pairs in a plait, making sewings to the beginning.

The lace is stiffened and mounted on the earrings.

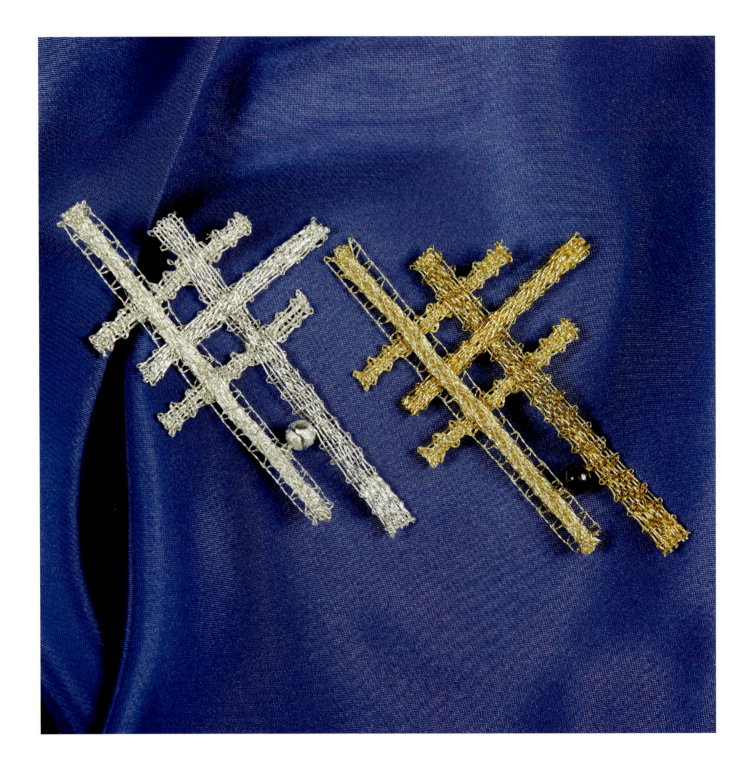

No. 15
Logs

Thread: Gold or Silver
Section 1, Lutac
Madeira Metallic Gold 3, Art.no. 9842 no. 40
(thin thread)

or Silver Art.no. 9842 no. 40
Madeira Metallic Gold Art.no. 9809 no. 12
(12 padding)

or Silver Art.no. 9809 no. 12

Section 2
Madeira Metallic Gold 43, Art.no. 9807 no. 6
(thick, shiny thread)

or Silver Art.no. 9807 no. 6
(passive pairs)

Madeira Metallic Gold 7, Art.no. 9842 no. 40
(thin thread)

or Silver Art.no. 9842 no. 40
(workers)

Section 3 and 5
Madeira Metallic Gold 33, Art.no. 9809 no. 12
or Silver Art.no. 9809 no. 12

Section 4
Madeira Metallic Gold 43, Art.no. 9807 no. 6
(thick, shiny thread) (passive pairs)

or Silver Art.no. 9807 no. 6
Madeira Metallic Gold 7, Art.no. 9842 no. 40
(workers)

or Silver Art.no. 9842 no. 40

1 of 4mm bead
1 brooch pin

Study the first working diagram.
All the logs are finished off with a helping thread because knots would be visible. See the detailed drawing page 7.

Working Diagram 1 - section 1
Use 7 pairs thin thread, with 3 as workers and 4 as passives. Work the Lutac base and leave the threads aside.

Working Diagram 2 - section 3 and 5
Work with 4 pairs 3ply thread and finish off.

Working Diagram 2 - section 4
Use 4 pairs thick shiny thread and I pair workers in thin thread. Work in linen stitch and finish off.

Working diagram 3 - section 1
Finish the Lutac section using 12 padding threads. Use 4 of the thin pairs to work half stitch over the padding. The remaining pairs continue in the padding. Work to the pin where the bead is added. At this point the thin pairs are laid aside. The lace is lightly stiffened. The pins are removed from section 4 and it is bent over backwards. Section 2 is then worked.

Working diagram 4 – section 2
Work in linen stitch with 4 pairs thick shiny thread (passives) and 1 worker pair of thin thread. Continue and add the bead as indicated (see the detailed diagram page 9). Complete section 2 and finish off. Fold section 4 back in place and stitch together where the logs overlap.

The lace is stiffened and mounted on a small brooch pin.

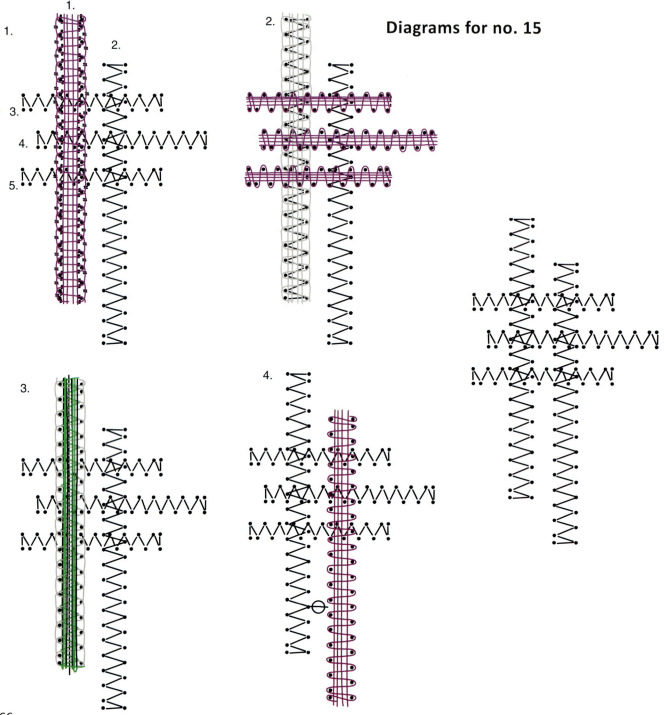

Diagrams for no. 15

Diagrams for no. 16

Begin

Section 1

Section 2

Begin

No. 16
Necklace with oval

Thread: Gold or Silver

Madeira Metallic Gold 7 Art.no. 9842 no. 40
(thin thread)

or

Silver Art.no. 9842 no. 40

Madeira Metallic Gold 33 Art.no. 9809 no. 12
(3ply)

or

Silver Art.no. 9809 no. 12

Madeira Metallic Gold 43 Art.no. 9807 no. 6
(thick shiny thread)

or

Silver Art.no. 9807 no. 6

Beads: 9 of 2½ mm

Section 1

Begin with 3 pairs thin thread and 1 pair 3ply on the first pin. Introduce 2 more pairs 3ply as in the working diagram. Finally add 1 pair thin thread as the last worker pair to the inner edge, altogether 3 worker pairs. Work past the pricking of section 2. The remainder of the band is worked later. The band is lightly stiffened and the pins are removed up to the corner to allow the band to be folded back.

Section 2

Begin adding pairs as follows: 2 pairs thin thread (workers), 1 pair thick shiny thread, 1 pair thin thread, 1 pair thick shiny thread and finally 1 pair thin thread (last worker pair). Follow the working diagram to the base of the oval (section 2). Lightly stiffen the lace and remove the pins from section 2 for ca. 1½ cm. The oval is folded back to allow the band of section 1 to be re-pinned past the first crossing of the bands. Be careful to use the correct pinholes. Re-pin and continue with the band of section 2, adding beads as indicated, and work past the next crossing of bands. Re-pin the remainder of section 1 over the oval and complete section 1.
Complete section 2, and the outermost 2 workers are plaited to section 1 and tied off.

Stiffen the lace and attach a ring at the top of the motif.

No. 16A

Earrings to match no 16

Thread: Gold or Silver

Madeira Metallic Gold 7 Art.no. 9842 no. 40
(thin thread)

or

Silver Art.no. 9842 no. 40

Madeira Metallic Gold 43 Art.no. 9807 no. 6
(thick, shiny thread)

or

Silver Art.no. 9807 no. 6

Beads: 9 of 2½ mm

Add the pairs as follows:
2 pairs thin thread (workers) 1 pair thick shiny thread, 1 pair thin thread, 1 pair thick shiny thread and finally 1 pair thin thread (last worker pair). Follow the working diagram. Remove 1 pair and complete the last half of the lace, adding beads as indicated. Finish by tying off the innermost pairs. The 2 outermost pairs of the oval form a plait, ca.1½ cm. A ring is mounted to the plait for attaching the earrings.

The lace is stiffened.

Diagrams for no. 16A

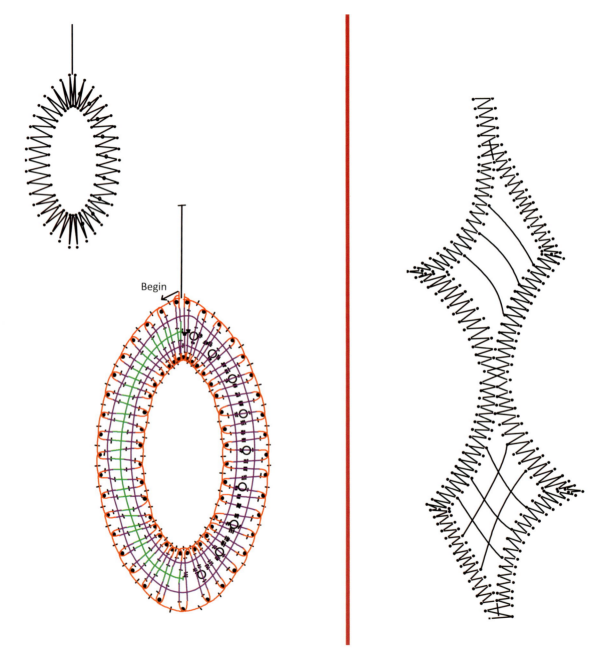

Begin

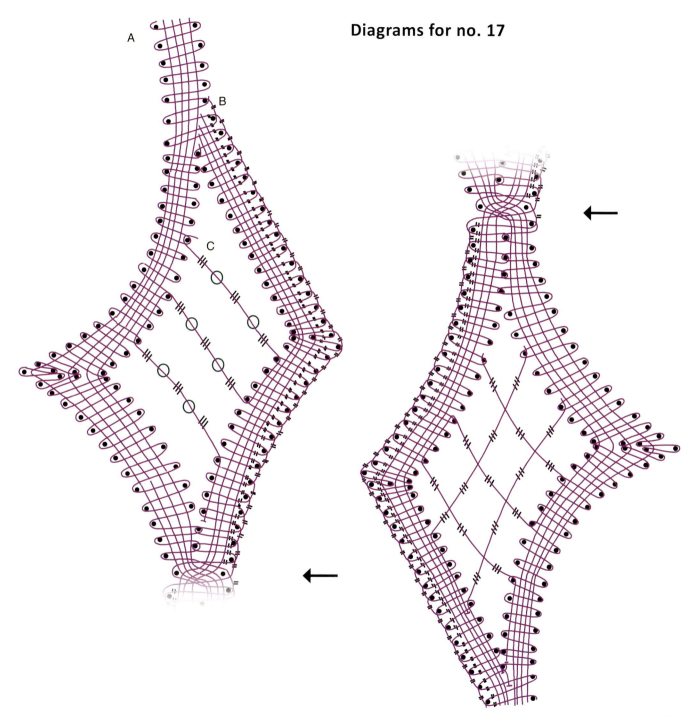

No. 17
Asymmetrical necklace

Thread: Gold or Silver
Madeira Metallic Gold 7, Art.no. 9842 no. 40
(thin thread)

or
Silver Art.no. 9842 no. 40

Madeira Metallic Gold 33, Art.no. 9809 no. 12
(3ply)

or
Silver Art.no. 9809 no. 12

Madeira Metallic Gold 43, Art.no. 9807 no. 6
(thick, shiny thread)

or
Silver Art.no. 9809 no. 6

6 of 3mm beads

Begin at A with 1 pair workers (thin thread) and 4 pairs passives (thick shiny thread). Follow the working diagram to B, where 5 pairs thin thread are added as indicated. Work each side separately. Add 1 pair of 3ply at C. The pair is twisted and beads are added as indicated.
At D the bands meet and cross as on the diagram, and the lace continues. 3 pairs of 3ply are added as filling for the lower section.
Remove pairs as indicated.

The threads are tied off and the lace is stiffened.

Fold the lace over the middle.
Fold over and stich the band in place at the top of the necklace to form a channel for the chain.

No. 18
Necklace of 2 crossed leaves

Thread: Gold or Silver
Madeira Metallic Gold 43, Art.no. 9807 no. 6
(thick, shiny thread)

or

Silver Art.no. 9807 no. 6

Madeira Metallic Gold 7, Art.no. 9842 no. 40
(workers and passive pairs)

or

Silver Art.no. 9842 no. 40

Plait: Gold 7, Art.no. 9842 no. 40
or
Silver, Art.no. 9842 no. 40 used double.

Metal thread in silver or gold: thickness ½ mm

Beads: 2 of 2mm beads and wire crimps.

Section 1
Attach a silver or gold metal thread to the pillow. Use 3 pairs gold/silver no. 40 (thin thread) and follow the working diagram. The outer pair is twisted twice and wound round the metal thread, which is kept in shape with pins. Complete section 1.
The pairs are wound around the metal thread and continue in section 2.

Section 2
The metal thread is laid on the left outermost edge so that it will lie in the middle of the leaf when it is turned. Add 2 pairs with double thread no. 40 (thin thread) to the plait on the outermost right edge. Then add 1 pair no.6 (thick shiny thread) together with the pairs from section 1. Add 2 more pairs as indicated. Turn at the tip and work the left side of the leaf in half stitch with whole stitch at the edge. Make sewings at the middle and around the metal thread.

Stiffen the lace and twist the metal thread to form a loop for the chain.

Attach 2 strings of beads, each with wire crimps and one bead. These are fixed to the top of the open leaf.

Diagrams for no. 18

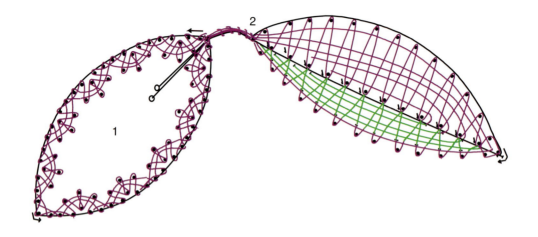

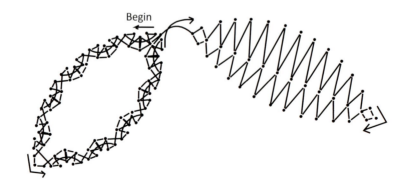

Diagrams for no. 18A

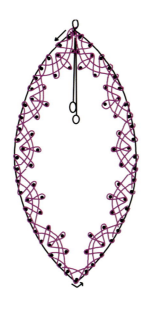

$\mathcal{N}o.$ 18A
Earrings to match no 18

Thread: Gold or Silver
Madeira Metallic Gold 43, Art.no. 9807 no. 6
(thick, shiny thread)

or
Silver Art.no. 9807 no. 6

Madeira Metallic Gold 7, Art.no. 9842 no. 40
(workers and passive pairs)

or
Silver Art.no. 9842 no. 40

Plait: Gold 7, Art.no. 9842 no. 40
or
Silver, Art.no. 9842 no. 40 used double.

Metal thread in silver or gold: thickness ½ mm

Beads: 2 of 2mm beads and wire crimps.

Fix the metal thread to the pillow. Follow the working diagram and work in linen stitch with 3 pairs gold/silver 40 (thin thread). Twist the outer pair twice and wind round the metal thread, which is kept in position with pins. To finish off, the metal thread is twisted to form a loop on to which the earrings are attached.

Attach 2 strings of beads, each with wire crimps and 1 bead. This is fixed at the top of the open leaf.

No. 19
Celtic Circle

Thread: Gold or Silver

Madeira Metallic Gold 7 Art.no. 9842 no. 40
(thin thread)

or

Silver Art.no. 9842 no. 40
(workers and passive pairs)

Madeira Metallic Gold 43 Art.no. 9807 no. 6
(thick, shiny thread)

or

Silver Art.no. 9807 no. 6
(gimp)

1 brooch pin

The inner oval bands are worked first and finished off leaving them open. After stiffening once, the pins are removed and the bands are plaited into each other as in the diagram. The finished plaited lace ovals are re-placed on the pricking and the outer ring is worked, making sewings to the ovals. Each band has 7 pairs. The passives and workers are in thin thread, and the gimp pairs are in thick shiny thread. The gimp is worked in chain stitch technique (see the detailed diagram page 12). Follow the working diagram.

Stiffen the lace again and mount on a brooch pin.

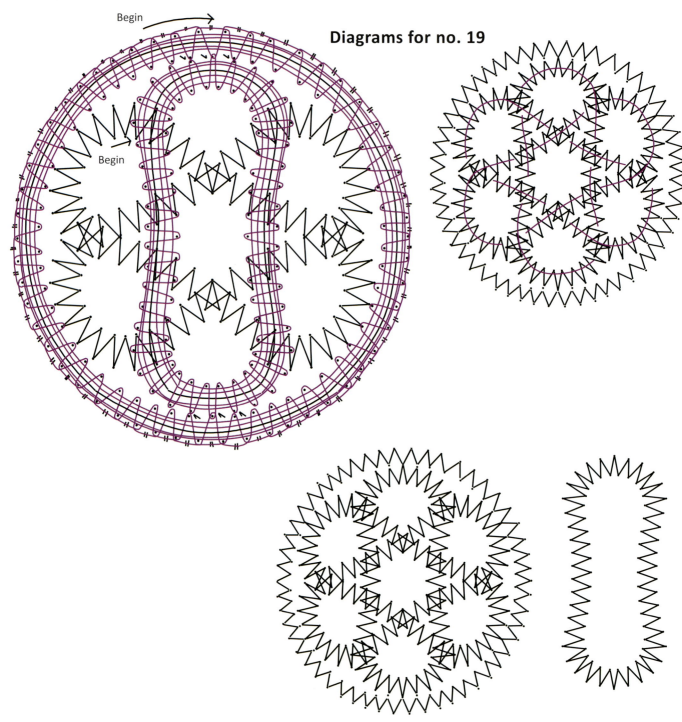

Begin

Begin

Diagrams for no. 19

Diagrams for no. 20

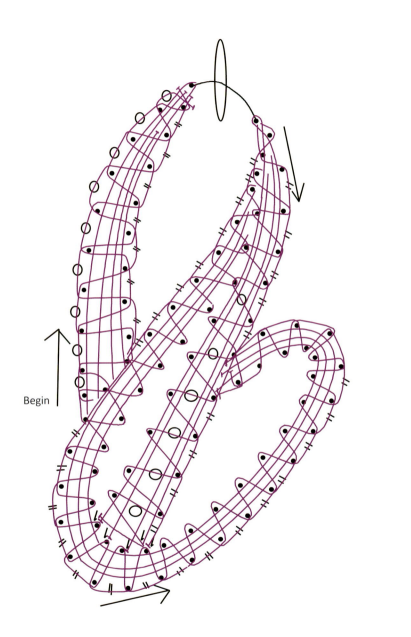

Begin

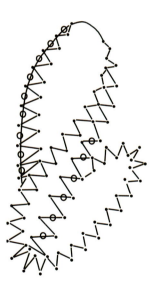

$\mathcal{N}$o. 20
Necklace

Thread: Gold or Silver
Madeira Metallic Gold Art.no. 9844 no. 30
(thin thread)

or
Silver Art.no. 9842 no. 40
(workers)

Madeira Metallic Silver Art.no. 9809 no. 12
(3ply) (passive pair)

Madeira Metallic Gold 43 Art.no. 9807 no. 6
(thick, shiny thread) (passive pairs)

Beads: 2 of 2mm beads and crimps

Begin with 1 pair silver workers and 1 pair 3ply on the first pin. On the next pin add 1 pair workers and 1 pair 3ply. Continue adding pairs as in the working diagram. The 3ply pair is a passive pair. Add beads as indicated. Remove pairs as indicated, and the last 2 pairs 3ply continue in a plait to the next part of the lace.

Add 2 worker pairs in thin thread and include the remaining 2 pairs from the plait as passives. Work to the 3rd pin where another 3ply pair is added. Continue to the 4th pin where another 3 ply pair is added. Work to the 5th pin and add a pair of thick shiny thread and 1 worker pair in gold on the left side. Add pairs of thick shiny thread as indicated on the left side. The band is then split so that the thick shiny thread continues in the left band and the 3ply thread continues in the right band. Follow the working diagram, and add beads as indicated. Remove pairs as indicated.

The lace is stiffened and a ring is mounted in the plait.